JOYS AND AGONIES

PRERNA DHINGRA

ISBN 979-888546036-1

I dedicate this book to all of my wonderful readers who are with
me in this journey and all those who would like to join.

Contents

Foreword

Sadness co-exists with joy. Be it sitting alone, away from all hustle-bustle, lack of support or disrespect from the humans around - emptiness can take over.

Nature can soothe this agony - not just plants, trees, the Sun, Moon, rivers, forest or animals but understanding from our fellow humans, their kindness, their healing words, their healing touch. We human beings need social contact in order to survive and thrive.

Unfortunately, we only see a little humanity at present and when we do, it warms our hearts.

This book is a short collection of poems, the initial part of which has light-hearted poems while the second part voices agonies of every aspect of our environment - from an individual to our planet Earth. I, along with my sister, would like to share yet another few poems and new moments with our readers.

-Prerna Dhingra

LIGHT HEARTED

1. Horror

I was all alone, inside my home,
but had someone, like no one.
They were phantom; they were with me,
standing at the door, blocking every path,
I was about to faint, maybe that was my bad luck.
The ghosts who dwelt here,
roamed here and there.
I had no way, that wasn't a play,
it was raining heavily,
the road was full of puddles,
I had no crucifix,
to make 'em fixed.
The house was dark,
there was no spark,
the story of this house was a mystery,
this house became lonely,
when I haunted it cruelly.

- Diya Dhingra

2. Night- a new bright

Night flies out,
but I can't count
the maze like stars,
though they were far.
May they come soon,
that will be a boon,
that star twinkles,
but soon I blink,
they fly aboard,
make me cry, like they abode.
But they are beautiful,
actually really bountiful,
they bring a new bright,
though making me wait
for a new night.

- Diya Dhingra

AGONIES

3. Fire

Beautiful sound, fire's creating,
orange, yellow, every few seconds, crackling,
with each sound all the same,
it revives from all the memories that drain
mind from harm, of life's asphyxia.
Against the feet, the soft touch of the grass,
against the cheek cool gusts,
it makes you forget all lust.
Peaceful slumber for the first
time on the bed inside the hut,
it's all covered in dust.
The feeling of being alone in this night,
speacial indeed, to stars I say goodnight,
wondering if I'm in heaven, I realise,
I spent my night here, saw beautiful sunrise
and saw all this beauty through my eyes.
- Prerna Dhingra

4. A Bullied Victim's Lament

"A little cool but tender breeze,
that is all I need to keep
my thundering mind full of peace.
Weather is perfectly divine,
enjoying it would be better
than drowning in any kind of grief of mine.
Through the Sun, a ray of hope shines,
that keeps me alive.
I can't do anything but think about all times,
when others used to look at me,
with those understanding eyes,
that used to betray all the lies.
Though it's hard to be sure whether 'twas genuine or fake,
anything good done to me now seems too late,
no one will ever know what makes my day.
It's after a long years of five I feel like,
something has pulled out a little of the knife
that's still stuck inside me, hurting me,
I want the cool shade of peaceful tree.
You are one of them or do you save me from those bulies?

I don't know, you mock me, but show care through your eyes,
it's fake or real; I don't want to know or even know,
whether to accept it or let it go.
It is hard to be sure whether this is a truth or lie,
that doesn't matter, I will remember it till the day I die."
- Prerna Dhingra

5. Cries Of A Girl Child

"Just after I was born,
my parents abandoned me,
to them was I like a thorn
or in their sight a flea?
Moments later on roadside I was lying,
layed on garbage pile, I was crying,
there arrived a hearty couple, they took me
to their home, they fed and took care of me,
they were different from the ones,
who didn't have the heart to know how their daughter was
doing.
Days passed by, fastly were the years passing,
one fine day, everyone was happy and enjoying,
the couple died and on the steets I started wondering.
Yet another day I saw dogs feeding on something,
I saw what it was; a little baby girl,
in my mind I thought:
Has something gone wrong?
If she's born a girl, is that her fault?"

- Prerna Dhingra

6. Cries Inside Virtual World

In front of the mobile,
clicking selfies with a smile,
pictures of chilling at the parties sipping, sipping wines,
wearing beautiful dresses with different hairstyles,
downloaded different apps,
is it called Instagram or Snapchat?
tap the keys of your PC,
no, I can't talk to you mum, I am busy.
Oblivious to others' agony,
while surfing websites titled "Sympathy"
lost inside the virtual world?
wait, isn't that a real world?
Dare not hide someone's mobile,
how will it's owner survive,
without their precious mobile?
some want maximum Youtube likes,
it's hard to resist dopamine,
why are we trying to win,
this never ending virtual fight?

- Prerna Dhingra

7. Earth's Agony

Hear children, ladies and gentlemen :
if it sounds good, do listen and understand,
humanity is dying and the Earth is crying,
we will do everything for the Earth we can,
we will try to co-operate and will never infuriate,
our helpless and poor mother.
For the sake of people and nature,
for tigers, whales and each other,
just try to offer each other your helping hand
and try to do whatever you can.

- Prerna Dhingra

www.ingramcontent.com/pod-product-compliance
Lightning Source LLC
Chambersburg PA
CBHW050744180726
48003CB00019B/1343